# How to Write a Book ASAP

## Workbook and Planning Guide

The step-by-step companion workbook to
*How to Write a Book ASAP:*
*A guide to writing your first book fast!*

Garrett Pierson

**How To Write A Book ASAP: Workbook and Planning Guide**

First published in 2011 by New Generation Consulting LLC.

ISBN-13: 978-0615576756

Printed in the United States of America

10 9 8 7 6 5 4 3 2 1

Creative Consultant, Editor and Typesetter:  **Susan D. Avery (Susan A., Elance.com/s/carlshaven/)**

Cover Design and Formatting:  **WebXGraphics (Elance.com/s/webxgraphics/)**

**John from Speedread (Elance.com/s/speedread)**

# Contents

# Chapter 1
# Ready, set, goal:
# Shift your mindset into gear!

**Ready...**

Have you ever considered what your particular mindset is about writing a book? You must have the right mindset in order to write a book. And, you must have these key ingredients:

- A well devised plan/goal that you are conscious about daily
- 100% commitment to that plan/goal
- Consistent desire and follow through of your plan/goal
- MOST IMPORTANT – determined mindset

**Set...**

Complete the self-assessment on the next page. This will give you an idea of where your mindset is now. This will give you a place to start in developing the mindset of a writer.

**Goal...**

You are going to begin writing your goals. Work through the steps that follow – each step will help you get started on your path to becoming an author!

**Set...Self-Assessment**

Answer the questions honestly in the self-assessment to see what your current mindset is for writing a book.

1.  Am I ready to take on the challenge of writing?

    _____

2.  Can I really do this?

    _____

3.  Do I enjoy reading? If so, what type of reading interests me?

    _____

4.  Am I worried about what others may think? If so, who?

    _____

5.  Do I possess enough knowledge on the subject I want to write about?

    _____

6.  What kind of doubts or worries do I have about writing a book?

    _____

    _____

    _____

    _____

7.  Am I afraid of not having enough time?

    _____

8.  Are there any other roadblocks that I can think of that are hindering me from writing?

    _____

    _____

    _____

9. Do I want to change any roadblocks and challenges into success?

_____

10. Can I see myself finishing a book?

_____

THE KEY – WORK QUICKLY
*Set a goal and commit yourself to it – you will triumph!*
*You are in control!*

**Goal...**

Let's get started. To begin, make sure you have read Chapter 1 of *How to Write a Book ASAP*.

Step 1: Write down your goals. Sit down and write down exactly what you want to accomplish. Be specific. First, try to fill in the blanks and then write out your own wording, making your goal your own.

- I am writing a book about _____ (Note: this can change as you work through this process)

- I will write at least a _____ page book

- I will find an accountability partner or coach to help me by _____(specific date)

- I will write/finish writing my book by _____(ex. September 15$^{th}$ 20** - be specific)

- I will write _____ pages per day or I will write _____ chapter(s) a week/month

- I will study/research for _____ minutes a day

- I will work on my claim (non-fiction) or building up the main character of my story (fiction) by _____(specific date)

- I will study my daily regimen and carve out the necessary time to write my book and will make my significant other and family aware of my goals by _____ (specific date)

**My Goal** in my own words:

_____

_____

_____

_____

_____

_____

_____

_____

_____

_____

_____

_____

_____

_____

_____

_____

_____

For more details on writing your goal, refer to *How to Write a Book ASAP*.

Step 2: Now that you have written down your goal, write down why you chose this goal – in other words, why you want to accomplish this.

_____

_____

_____

_____

_____

_____

Step 3: You need a strategic plan to accomplish your goals. Write down milestones with target dates that will help you accomplish your goals. Be realistic and go with your first impressions.

_____

_____

_____

_____

_____

_____

_____

_____

_____

Step 4: Create a binding agreement with yourself. On the line below, sign and date your goal, making a binding contract for yourself. Then tell someone else about it and take a 'power walk', focusing on how to fulfill your contract and meet your goals.

Signature: _____ Date: _____

*Commit – Reorganize your time – Believe that you can finish – Focus on finishing!*

# NOTES

# Chapter 2
# Start Writing – What?

The most important part of any journey is reaching your destination. You now have established a goal for your writing – that is your destination. Now is the time to decide exactly what you plan to write about. Are you writing fiction, a novel, poetry, or non-fiction? It is better to select a topic that is comfortable and familiar, rather than a topic you are unfamiliar with requiring a lot of extra time-consuming research.

The exercises in this chapter will help you narrow down your choices for writing your book.

What is the purpose of my book?

What type of book will it be?

What is my topic?

When should I begin?

You are going to think about the "Where", "Why", "What" and "When" so that you can move on to "How" to start writing. The book you are writing must be something you believe you can write and it must be aligned with your goals. Let's get started!

**Purpose of Book**

It is important to understand the purpose of your book. Below you will find an image/diagram which can help get the juices flowing in your mind as to what the purpose of your book will be. Once you understand the purpose of your book you will be able to proceed on the road to writing your book. As you look at the diagram, jot down any notes or thoughts you may have for the direction of your book.

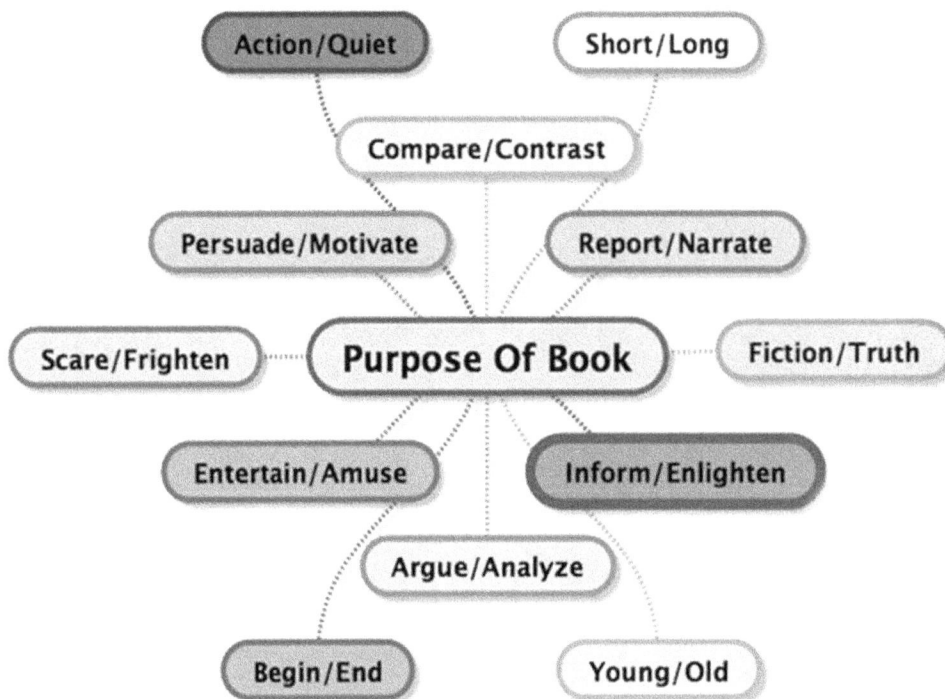

Notes:

_____

_____

_____

_____

_____

_____

## Type of Book

Check one:

☐ I am interested in writing fiction.

Type: _____

☐ I am interested in writing non-fiction.

Type: _____

☐ I am interested in writing _____.

Type: _____

## Topic Choices

Take a moment and write down the different topics you have considered writing on. Then, make sure that your topic choices align with your goals.

_____

_____

_____

_____

Look at the choices below. If you are having trouble deciding on your topic, give your choices the test below. If you can check the box next to each of these statements, indicating that you agree with the statement regarding your topic choice, then you have a winning topic.

☐ You feel a sense of urgency to write about the subject at hand

☐ You can visualize the book in your hands

☐ You can easily articulate to others what your book will be about

☐ The subject and/or characters come easy to you, even naturally

☐ Putting together a one paragraph (and no more) description of your book takes you less than two minutes

☐ You not only believe that you can write about this subject, you know you can

☐ You feel confident that people will learn or be entertained by its content

☐ You can create content that is unique on the subject, and/or you can tell unique stories that relate to the reader and the subject

☐ You feel there is a need for your take on the subject/story in your market/niche

☐ You feel obligated to write about this topic or theme

☐ You will write until you are finished

*NOW is the right time! NOW is the right time!*

Let's visualize your journey and destination for a minute. Take a few moments to ponder each of these questions. Adequate room has been made for you to take notes of any thoughts you may want to jot down here.

**Where** are you going?

_____

_____

_____

_____

**Why** are you going there?

_____

_____

_____

**What** are you going to do to get there?

_____

_____

_____

_____

**When** are you going to start?

_____

_____

_____

_____

Once you have answered these questions and worked through them, you are ready to move on to HOW you are going to write your book fast!

*Demand excellence from yourself and you will obtain brilliance.*

Note:

Please read Chapter 2 of *How to Write a Book ASAP* if you have not done so already. It contains the base information used in this workbook to help you on your way.

If you need additional help writing a novel or short story, visit HowToWriteABookASAP.com/jeff to find out more about how Jeff Gerke's program can help you.

If you need additional help writing a non-fiction or "how-to" book, I suggest you learn more about my full platinum training program at HowToWriteABookASAP.com/training.

# NOTES

# Chapter 3
# Strategies for Organization

While it may be true that a writer can think up new ideas as soon as pen hits paper, it is not necessarily the case. Writing takes organization and self-control. Writing takes research, thought, revision, practice, and time management.

How can you learn about the writing styles of others? By reading!

How can you learn your own writing style? By writing!

*Time management is essential.*

Making the time to write is imperative. Set aside some time every day to write. Although there are only 24 hours in every day, there is likely a small block of time that you can commit to writing your book every day. Perhaps you could give up some time in front of the television or playing video games. Or, perhaps you could get up a little earlier. This would add a few more minutes to your day, but aren't you worth it?

The table on the following page is taken from *How to Write a Book ASAP*, Chapter 3. Take the time to fill out the schedule so that you can see where your time goes. You may be surprised by how much or how little time you have to spare. Either way, you will be able to form an educated plan once you know how your current schedule looks.

Finally, make sure that you begin and commit to follow the Seven Step Commitment Plan given in this chapter. If, after going through the exercises in this chapter, you need to adjust your goals in Chapter 1, then by all means go back and make the adjustments now so that you stay focused on finishing!

**Time Management Table**

The Time Management Table divides each day of the week into 30 minute increments. First, fill in the table on the next page by writing down everything that you do regularly on a daily basis. (You may also download a table like this from HowToWriteABookASAP.com/schedule.)

After you fill in the table, look at the table and begin highlighting or crossing through non-essential activities. Note: 'non-essential' activities are those that are not required for your innermost happiness. Essential activities are mostly associated with family, community and employment. Cross through things that aren't making a significant impact for the betterment of your life.

Once you have completed this exercise, you should have a good idea of when you can make the time to write. You may have some wasted time or you may have a tight schedule. By discovering now how much time you can commit, you are another step closer to being an author!

After working through this chart, write down when the best times are to work on your writing:

_____

_____

_____

_____

_____

| | Sunday | Monday | Tuesday | Wednesday | Thursday | Friday | Saturday |
|---|---|---|---|---|---|---|---|
| 12am | | | | | | | |
| 12:30 | | | | | | | |
| 1:00 | | | | | | | |
| 1:30 | | | | | | | |
| 2:00 | | | | | | | |
| 2:30 | | | | | | | |
| 3:00 | | | | | | | |
| 3:30 | | | | | | | |
| 4:00 | | | | | | | |
| 4:30 | | | | | | | |
| 5:00 | | | | | | | |
| 5:30 | | | | | | | |
| 6:00 | | | | | | | |
| 6:30 | | | | | | | |
| 7:00 | | | | | | | |
| 7:30 | | | | | | | |
| 8:00 | | | | | | | |
| 8:30 | | | | | | | |
| 9:00 | | | | | | | |
| 9:30 | | | | | | | |
| 10:00 | | | | | | | |
| 10:30 | | | | | | | |
| 11:00 | | | | | | | |
| 11:30 | | | | | | | |
| 12pm | | | | | | | |
| 12:30 | | | | | | | |
| 1:00 | | | | | | | |
| 1:30 | | | | | | | |
| 2:00 | | | | | | | |
| 2:30 | | | | | | | |
| 3:00 | | | | | | | |
| 3:30 | | | | | | | |
| 4:00 | | | | | | | |
| 4:30 | | | | | | | |
| 5:00 | | | | | | | |
| 5:30 | | | | | | | |
| 6:00 | | | | | | | |
| 6:30 | | | | | | | |
| 7:00 | | | | | | | |
| 7:30 | | | | | | | |
| 8:00 | | | | | | | |
| 8:30 | | | | | | | |
| 9:00 | | | | | | | |
| 9:30 | | | | | | | |
| 10:00 | | | | | | | |
| 10:30 | | | | | | | |
| 11:00 | | | | | | | |
| 11:30 | | | | | | | |

**Setting Length and Target Date**

Now that you know how much time you have to write your book, let's look at the length of your book and how much time it will take to write it.

Right now, you need to come up with a rough estimate of how long you would like for your book to be. A non-fiction book should be 100+ pages and a novel should be 200+ pages. The average book size is 5.5 x 8.5 inches. This works out to about 80 pages in Microsoft Word to equal roughly 120 pages of a 5.5 x 8.5 inch book.

Refer to Chapter 2 of *How to Write a Book ASAP* for more information on setting the length of your book.

Write down your goal here:

My goal is to write a _____ page book.

Now that you have the estimated length of your book, you can figure on how much time it will take to write it. You can fill in the blanks to complete the formula below for your book, or you can use the online calculator that I have created so that you can easily do the math. Simply go to HowToWriteABookASAP.com/calculator. If you use the calculator online, remember to come back here and write in your times.

Formula:

*(# of pages you want your book to be ÷ 1.5) x average time that it takes you to write one normal full MSWord document page in minutes ÷ 60 = hours of writing needed to finish book*

> Example: I want to write a 120 page book. I can write one normal full MSWord document page in about 35 minutes on average.
>
> 120 ÷ 1.5 = 80 pages
> 80 x 35 = 2800 minutes
> 2800 ÷ 60 = **47** hours of writing to finish my book
>
> So let's say that it takes me 47 hours to write my book. If I write 30 minutes a day, then it will take me 70.5 days of writing to finish my book. If I write for 2 hours a day then I could finish my book in 23.5 days.

Now it's your turn...

Your calculation:

Number of pages you estimate for your book: _____ ÷ 1.5 = _____

Answer: _____ ÷ minutes to write normal page _____ = _____

Answer: _____ ÷ 60 = _____ hours of writing needed to finish your book.

So, it will take you _____ hours to write your book. You plan to write _____

minutes/hours per day. It will take you _____ days to finish your book.

Therefore, your targeted date for finishing your book is _____.

Simply go to HowToWriteABookASAP.com/calculator. If you use the calculator online, remember to come back here and write your times in the spaces provided.

*Writing involves planning. When you organize your time to write,*
*you have given yourself the opportunity to arrange your thoughts.*
*That is when the real writing begins!*

**Seven Step Commitment Plan**

The Seven Step Commitment Plan helps you to commit to a plan so that you can begin writing. Go through the steps in the plan below to see if you are ready to start writing. There will be more help in upcoming chapters, so if you can't follow through yet on each of the items for this plan, come back to this chapter and complete it when you are ready. Remember, make sure that your goals in Chapter 1 are updated to reflect any changes that you make.

1) Commit to finishing the book by a specific date (write your target date here)

_____

2) Form a specific page/chapter/topic plan and goals (write these down)

_____

_____

_____

_____

_____

_____

_____

_____

3) Commit to a subject/storyline (write what you have decided on here)

_____

_____

_____

_____

_____

4) Construct a title for your book (write your title here – you can change it later)

_____

5) Create chapter titles for book – after completing the exercises in Chapter 5 of this workbook, make a note here that you have completed this exercise. Make additional notes as needed.

_____

_____

_____

_____

_____

_____

6) Create simple outlines for each chapter – after completing the outlines exercise in Chapter 5 of this workbook, make a note here that you have completed this exercise. Make additional notes as needed.

_____

_____

_____

_____

_____

_____

_____

7) Stick to your word!

The first 3 should have already been done by now. Numbers 4, 5 and 6 are new, yet you will learn more about these steps as you progress through the workbook.

When you have completed the 7 steps, then you can commit yourself to starting. Make sure you read Chapter 3 in *How to Write a Book ASAP* for further help with these exercises.

*You need to have a very solid and specific goal on your start date to begin writing.*
*Once you get the ball rolling it will be hard to stop it.*

# NOTES

---

---

---

---

---

---

---

---

---

---

---

---

---

---

---

---

---

---

---

---

---

# Chapter 4
# All the Right Ingredients

There are several ingredients for having success as a writer. Here is a breakdown of what we have learned so far:

Chapter 1: Key ingredients to your success:

- A well devised plan/goal that you are conscious about daily
- 100% commitment to that plan/goal
- Consistent desire and follow through of your plan/goal
- MOST IMPORTANT – precise mindset

Chapter 2: What is it that you want to write about? Do you feel a sense of urgency to write it?

Chapter 3: Time management is vital. Have you decided on the length of your book and figured out the amount of time it will take to write it? Have you updated your goals in Chapter 1?

The exercises in this chapter will help you find answers to some questions you may have, while providing you with additional ingredients that will help ensure your writing success.

## The Big 5

There are 5 core questions that are asked by most potential writers. Go back and reread Chapter 4 in *How to Write a Book ASAP*. After reading the five questions and my answers to them, write down your thoughts in the spaces below. This exercise will help the answers become more real to you.

1. How and where do I start?

\
\
\
\
\

2. In what type of style should I write my book? Simple or technical?

\
\

3. How long should my book be?

\

4. First person vs. third person?

\

5. Can I write a book without good writing skills?

\
\
\
\

Still have questions? Go to: HowToWriteABookASAP.com/questions

**Research**

Research is important for any writer. You must know your topic. Below are some resources that are useful for research. Additional space is given for you to list additional resources that would be helpful for you to use in your research. This will give you "tools" that you can use for writing.

Magazines

Videos

Articles

News/Hot Topics

University Studies

Kids (you'd be surprised)

Asking people questions (surveys and polls)

Forums/Message boards

"Words That Sell" a book by Richard Bayan

_____

_____

_____

_____

_____

Research Notes:

_____

_____

_____

_____

**Self-Control**

Distracted thinking is where your mind gets easily sidetracked and lacks focus. On the other hand, controlled thinking is organized and has a purpose (taken from Chapter 5 of *How to Write a Book ASAP* – read it if you haven't already!)

Let's look at the benefits of training your mind to think in a specifically controlled manner:

- Controlled thinking enables you to become the master of your own mind. You achieve this by learning to control your emotions and thought patterns.

- It will motivate you to work with a well-defined goal or objective.

- It supports and develops the mind as it relates to the practice of working with a clear plan.

- It improves your self-assurance.

- It allows you to arouse the subconscious mind optimistically to greater actions, in achievement of a defined objective – giving you the power you need to remove negative, damaging beliefs.

- It helps you to acquire the pattern of making correct analysis through which you can uncover solutions to your problems instead of fretting over the roadblocks you may have. The act of discovering the solutions to challenges provides peace of mind.

- It develops a creative mind rather than a lazy mind. A creative mind leads to success, where a lazy or distracted mind leads to lack of action or worse, misguided action.

- Controlled thoughts offer you a more organized life.


Before moving on to the next exercise, pause for a moment. Reread each of the benefits listed above. Write down any notes that come to your mind below. How do you feel about this?

_____

_____

_____

_____

_____

_____

**Five Steps to Gaining Control**

Below you will find questions that align with each of the five steps to gaining control. Answer the questions, making sure to take notes as you go. You really want to "get" this.

1.  *Think with a purpose.*
    What motivates you and inspires you?

    _____

    _____

    _____

    _____

    _____

    _____

    _____

2.  *Time to concentrate.*
    This exercise should be done daily. For now, give it a try. Find a place to be alone for at least five minutes. Clear your mind and ponder what you want or need. Set goals and/or concentrate on your goals. Don't focus on the details – just focus on results. After doing this exercise, return here and write down your thoughts.

    _____

    _____

    _____

    _____

    _____

    _____

    _____

3. *Get the facts.*
   Make sure you have reliable information. Some websites, for example, are simply not trustworthy. You need facts to connect to your purpose – this will be an aid in writing. Based on the type of book you have determined to write, what are some facts that you may need to research further? Where might you look to find trustworthy information?

   _____

   _____

   _____

   _____

   _____

   _____

   _____

   _____

4. *Take note of your thoughts.*
   Do you feel as if you become distracted easily? Sometimes it is a matter of prioritizing. If you find that you are distracted, take a moment to realize that you are, indeed, distracted. Take note of it. Write down any thoughts that are distracting you. Once you have written them down, take note of them so that they will no longer be distractions in the future.

   _____

   _____

   _____

   _____

   _____

   _____

   _____

5.  *Be realistic.*
    Read over everything you have written down in these five steps. On the lines below,
    group any interrelated thoughts together, showing their connectedness. You are
    organizing what you have written in the first four steps – keep it simple.

    _____

    _____

    _____

    _____

    _____

    _____

    _____

    _____

    _____

    _____

    _____

    _____

    _____

Are you inspired and motivated to finish? Are you really ready to start?

Now the journey begins for you to write and finish your book!

*The mind is a powerful tool that when used correctly can
solve any problem, overcome any obstacle and write any book.*

# NOTES

# Chapter 5
# The Writing Process:
# You Can Do It!

Any time you travel on a journey, you will need a map to get to your destination. A map helps you find your way to your destination; much like blueprints can help a contractor build a home. In much the same way, you need to form a core for your writing that will lead you to your destination – a finished book. You may be asking yourself, what is the core? The core consists of the basic components of a book. As we work through the exercises in this chapter, you will learn more about forming the core of your book and working on the development of each part.

If you haven't done so yet, read Chapters 6 and 7 of *How to Write a Book ASAP* to get more in-depth information to aid in your exercises for this chapter.

As you finish each component of your core, you will come to a significant point in the creation process of your book. Your core will be finished and suddenly your book has become a reality in your mind. You have made a psychological shift! Why? When you have the core and a created cover for your book, you have an incredible motivational tool for you to finish writing your book. Keep the cover of your book in front of you. Envision the final book. You will get there!

## THE CORE

There are four important elements that form the core of your book and it is important to do them all. These elements are:

Book Title and Subtitle
Cover (front and back)
Chapter Titles
Chapter Outlines

Roll up your sleeves as we go to work on each of these core elements.

### Book Title and Subtitle

Take a full day to develop your book title. Without a title, you don't have a book. If you desire a subtitle (good for non-fiction, rare for fiction), now is the time to develop this as well. Pull together your research. Next, write down anything that comes to your mind, making a whole list of possible titles. You can ask others for suggestions. You can search by keyword (detailed in book on page 75) or start looking at book titles online. Get those creative juices going. Then, write your ideas below.

_____

_____

_____

_____

_____

_____

_____

_____

_____

_____

_____

Write down in one paragraph what your book is about. Simply sit down and write one paragraph. No more than one paragraph – this exercise is not to be burdensome.

_____

_____

_____

_____

_____

_____

Did you come up with additional title ideas after writing your paragraph? If so, write them here:

_____

_____

_____

_____

Finally, pick your best title. You can change your mind later, but for now, go ahead and pick the best title. Do the same for the subtitle, if you plan to use one.

*Title:*

_____

*Subtitle:*

_____

**Cover (front and back)**

Make sure you have read Chapter 7 of *How to Write a Book ASAP*. Once you have read that chapter, you will understand this section better. Here was my cover idea as a wireframe model from my book:

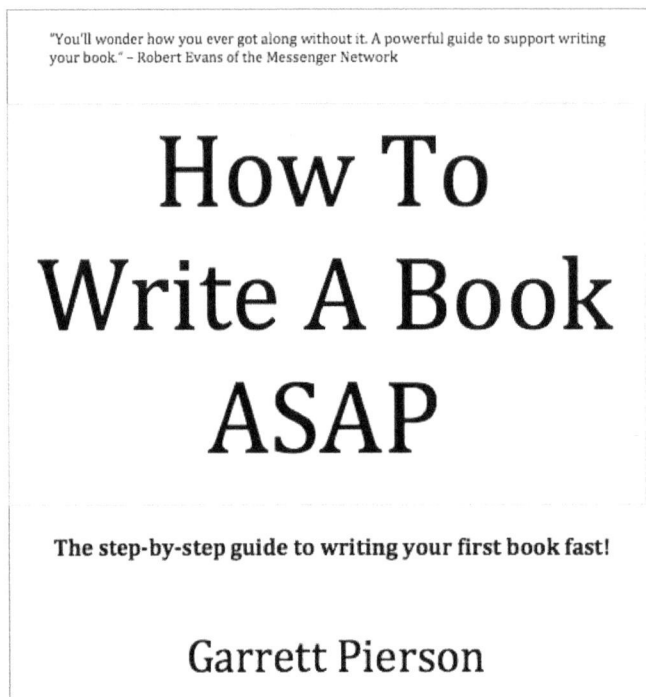

Take out a few sheets of regular notebook paper. Try out some ideas for your cover. After all, you know who you are (the author). You have chosen a title (and possible subtitle). After playing with your own ideas, follow the suggestions in Chapter 7 to make your cover a reality. Especially pay attention to the information given for outsourcing your cover design. Write down any notes here that you need to remember as you go through this process.

_____

_____

_____

_____

_____

**Chapter Titles**

Chapter titles can serve as a way to orient and control your reader's interest level and expectations. Your chapter titles need to be short and to the point. Remember, they are there to guide you as you write.

Note: some types of books do not use chapter titles. If your book does not use chapter titles, then perhaps jot down the main idea of each chapter or section of your book.

It may be hard to just sit down and come up with chapter titles. However, by brainstorming ideas with what you plan to write in your book, you should be able to come up with titles that reflect what you are planning to write about.

For example, let's say you are writing a book on horse racing. What is it you wish to say about horse racing? Are you going to discuss specific races or the types of horses used in the races? Will this be a book from an insider's view or from a spectator's view? Let's say that you settle on writing about specific horse races like the Kentucky Derby, the Preakness, the Belmont Stakes, the Breeder's Cup, etc. You have to research each of these races to come up with the information you will use for your book. You could separate your chapters by one race per chapter, giving you an idea of what to use for a chapter title. The chapter on the Kentucky Derby could be called "Kentucky's Most Famous Two Minutes" or "The Great Race at Churchill Downs" or something uniquely yours that fits what you will write about.

Caution: Do not use someone else's ideas and do not use a trademark or slogan. Make sure that your chapter titles are your own original work – this applies to content also.

Okay, so let's get started on some ideas.

First, on the first line below write out the title to your book again (it never hurts to see it, does it?) Then, under the title, begin writing out ideas for how you would like your book to develop. You should have an idea in your mind of where you would like to start and begin building on that. You are not writing the book here, just ideas for what chapters you may want to include in your book. Consult Chapter 6 in *How to Write a Book ASAP* if you need more ideas on how to accomplish this.

Title: _____

Chapter Title ideas:

_____

_____

_____

_____

_____

_____

_____

_____

_____

_____

_____

_____

_____

Good, you now have some ideas for your chapter titles. These titles can be changed as you go, but at least you have a starting idea. Now we move on to one of the most important exercises you will do for your book. Don't give up here – keep going! You are creating a masterpiece!

**Chapter Outlines**

You have chosen a title and you have worked on chapter titles. It is time to start developing what you want to say in each chapter. This is an integral part of the process. You want to have a clear vision of what you are going to write and the best way to accomplish this is to make a chapter outline. This gives you an abbreviated summary to keep you on track as you write. It doesn't matter what type of book you are writing – fiction or non-fiction – it is important to have an outline to allow you to make decisions for what goes where in your book.

So what should you focus on when creating your chapter outlines? From *How to Write a Book ASAP*:

While creating your chapter outline here are some things to focus on:

- Do you have the main idea and supporting details?

- Highlight the important points you plan to focus on.

- What is the purpose of the chapter?

- What is your viewpoint or the viewpoint of the character(s)?

- Ask yourself: who, what, where, when and why?

- What information do you need to gather via research?

- Arrange your information in a logical order. For example, you can start from the most to least important, in the order you see the chapter going, chronologically, by character or by scene.

The way you organize the chapter outline may serve as a model for how you further divide and write the book.

One important thing to remember: your chapter outlines should be no longer than a page – make them short and sweet.

Several pages are given here for you to work on your chapter outlines. You may also photocopy additional pages, if needed. If you are comfortable with mind mapping, as explained in Chapter 6 of *How to Write a Book ASAP*, feel free to work through the process that way. Please do not skip this step – it is vital to writing your first book fast!

Chapter Title: _____

Outline:

_____

_____

_____

_____

_____

_____

_____

_____

_____

_____

_____

_____

_____

_____

_____

_____

_____

_____

_____

_____

_____

_____

_____

_____

Chapter Title: _____

Outline:

_____

_____

_____

_____

_____

_____

_____

_____

_____

_____

_____

_____

_____

_____

_____

_____

_____

_____

_____

Chapter Title: _____

Outline:

_____

_____

_____

_____

_____

_____

_____

_____

_____

_____

_____

_____

_____

_____

_____

_____

_____

_____

_____

_____

_____

Chapter Title: _____

Outline:

_____

_____

_____

_____

_____

_____

_____

_____

_____

_____

_____

_____

_____

_____

_____

_____

_____

_____

_____

Chapter Title: _____

Outline:

Chapter Title: _____

Outline:

_____

_____

_____

_____

_____

_____

_____

_____

_____

_____

_____

_____

_____

_____

_____

_____

_____

_____

_____

_____

_____

Chapter Title: _____

Outline:

_____

_____

_____

_____

_____

_____

_____

_____

_____

_____

_____

_____

_____

_____

_____

_____

_____

_____

Chapter Title: _____

Outline:

_____

_____

_____

_____

_____

_____

_____

_____

_____

_____

_____

_____

_____

_____

_____

_____

_____

_____

Chapter Title: _____

Outline:

_____

_____

_____

_____

_____

_____

_____

_____

_____

_____

_____

_____

_____

_____

_____

_____

_____

_____

_____

Chapter Title: _____

Outline:

_____

_____

_____

_____

_____

_____

_____

_____

_____

_____

_____

_____

_____

_____

_____

_____

_____

_____

_____

*Any tool that can help motivate you and*
*keep you motivated is one that you should fully embrace!*

# NOTES

# Chapter 6
# Finishing Your Book Fast!

By this time you should be making great progress towards finishing your book. Now is the time to write, write, write. Stick to your schedule and don't give up! Remember the time you set aside in your schedule to write? Try to stick to it. Avoid distractions.

If you haven't read Chapter 8 in *How to Write a Book ASAP*, then now is the time. Read it through carefully as you get ready to embark on your journey.

You may use any method you wish to write your book. By computer, by hand or spoken, it doesn't matter – don't get caught up in the method. The point is to stay focused on your goal and just write, write, write.

There are many ideas for effective writing. However, it ultimately comes down to these five main points:

1. A Congruent Beginning, Middle and End

2. A Main Idea

3. Effective Description Incorporating Emotion

4. A Well-defined and Meaningful Purpose/Plot

5. Consistent Tone and Flow

In most cases, it doesn't matter if the writing is non-fiction, fiction, essay, press release, blog post, or anything else that you are writing – these are the basic components.

There are also coaches and courses available to help with your writing.

- If you want to write a novel, I suggest Jeff Gerke's course that you can access here – HowToWriteABookASAP.com/novel-course

- If you want an effective way to write a non-fiction book then I suggest my training course. You can learn more about it here – HowToWriteABookASAP.com/non-fiction-course

The only exercise necessary for this chapter is for you to write. Don't delay – get started right now! You are ready to write your first book fast!

*Your location and mindset will not only affect the way you write.*
*It will also affect how fast you write.*

# NOTES

# Chapter 7
# Getting Your Book Published

You have worked very hard to write your book. Hours have been spent researching, organizing and writing. Now what? Where do you go from here?

For starters, please make sure you read Chapter 9 of *How to Write a Book ASAP*. Decisions have to be made at this point and much of the information you need to make informed decisions are found in this chapter.

There are two basic routes to getting your book published: traditional publishing or self publishing. Carefully consider this decision based on what you have read in my book.

If you choose traditional publishing, then I advise caution, research and a lot of tenacity. Every aspect of traditional publishing is up to the publisher; therefore, no two writers will have exactly the same experience. There are also no guarantees that your book will get published.

However, let me steer you instead towards self publishing. Self publishing is a process that we can work through together. It may mean more work, but it will get you published. After all, what good is a book if it never gets published?

The exercises in this chapter will help you on your way to getting your book published. Take it step-by-step to reach your goals.

Let's get started so you can get finished!

## STEPPING STONES

The steps outlined for these exercises are the exact steps I use to self publish. Follow through the steps and make sure to take notes and make your own plan as you go.

Step 1: **Write the Book**

Do you have a rough draft of your book yet? If not, get back to it and return here when you have at least finished your rough draft.

Date rough draft finished: _____

Step 2: **Find a Proofreader**

Choose one or two people that you trust and that have adequate use of the language you are writing in. Give them copies of your rough draft (paper or digital file) and ask them to return it to you with any corrections (their opinion) by a certain date. Fill in below as you go:

Proofreader #1 Name: _____

I gave my rough draft to this person on _____ (date).

I asked them to return the corrected draft to me on _____ (date).

Proofreader #2 Name: _____

I gave my rough draft to this person on _____ (date).

I asked them to return the corrected draft to me on _____ (date).

It is good if the person proofreading openly gives you constructive criticism. That will help you the most in the long run.

Date returned: _____

Step 3: **Rewrite if Needed**

Consider the suggestions that your proofreader(s) gave you. Then rewrite anything that needs reworking. Start from the beginning of your manuscript and read it through. Sometimes it helps to read it out loud. If it doesn't make sense to you when you read it, it won't make sense to your intended audience.

Date rewrite complete: _____

Step 4: **Hire a Copy Editor**

This should be outsourced as described in my book. Please follow my suggestions in *How to Write a Book ASAP* so that you choose a quality copy editor. The copy editor is responsible for checking grammar and spelling, as well as making any edits so that the book will flow better. This is best left to someone with experience.

Name of copy editor I will use: _____

Date submitted manuscript to copy editor: _____   Cost: _____

Deadline for copy editor to return manuscript: _____

Date edited manuscript received: _____

Step 5: **Create Additional Pages**

Once you have received the final edited version of your book it is time to create the following additional pages. Place a check in the box next to those you will be creating.

- ☐ Title cover page
- ☐ Copyright page
- ☐ Table of contents

The following are optional but can be helpful additions to your book:

- ☐ About the author
- ☐ List of figures
- ☐ List of tables
- ☐ Dedication
- ☐ Acknowledgments
- ☐ Foreword
- ☐ Preface
- ☐ Introduction
- ☐ Appendix
- ☐ Glossary
- ☐ Index
- ☐ Notes
- ☐ Bibliography

Date additional pages complete: _____

Step 6: **Find a Printer**

This is another area where you have many options. Again, please consult Chapter 9 of *How to Write a Book ASAP* for guidance in this area.

Name of Printer: _____

Date delivered to printer: _____

Notes regarding printing:

_____

_____

_____

_____

_____

_____

_____

Step 7: **Get an ISBN Number and Barcode**

My ISBN Number: _____

Date ISBN and Barcode completed: _____

Step 8: **Hire a Typesetter**

This is another area which should be outsourced. Please follow the recommendations given in my book. The typesetter will take your manuscript (either whole or in different chapter files) and typeset only – formatting for printing with page numbers, headers and footers.

Additional proofreading at this point will be an extra cost. Also, any changes that the typesetter has to go back and correct will involve more cost. You can either make sure it is right when you submit, or choose a typesetter that can also proofread your manuscript one last time (with a fresh pair of eyes). The extra proofreading adds to your cost but ensures that your manuscript is ready to go to the printer. If you just pay for typesetting alone, your typesetter will not read over your manuscript – it will be set as is. The typesetter must be able to follow the printer's guidelines for the final product. My typesetter, Susan D. Avery (Susan A., Elance.com/s/carlshaven/), produces a .pdf document ready for the printer that I can keep and submit for printing.

Typesetter's Name: _____

Date manuscript sent to typesetter: _____ Cost: _____

Deadline date for final document from typesetter: _____

Date received final document from typesetter: _____

Final number of pages (after typesetting – you will need this for printing and spine): _____

## Step 9: **Finalize Cover Design (front, back, spine)**

It is time to look at your book cover again. You worked on this a few chapters back, but now it is time to complete the job. In addition to your front cover, you will need a back cover and a spine designed. Once again, make sure you read this section of Chapter 9 in *How to Write a Book ASAP*. I give helpful guidelines to make this easier.

Cover Designer's Name: _____

Date cover designer begins: _____ Cost: _____

Deadline date for completed cover: _____

Date received completed project: _____

## Step 10: **Submit all Required Files to Printer**

You have carefully done everything up to this point. Make sure to get a proof (either digital .pdf, printed or both) so that you can double check everything before it goes into full print.

Date sent to printer: _____

Date received proof: _____

Date for final books to arrive: _____

That's it! You have written your book and now you have the tools to finish it! Only one more chapter left to go for ideas on how to market your book.

Note:
This chapter could bring up various concerns or questions all of which can be answered at HowToWriteABookASAP.com/questions. Also, be sure to take advantage of my step-by-step online training course if you haven't done so already. I go into much more detail on how to self publish or get your book published.

*You will feel the pleasure of accomplishment and fully experience the power
and authority that comes from being able to say that you are an author.*

# NOTES

# Chapter 8
# Closing the Book on Your Book:
# A New Beginning

There it sits – right in front of you – your first book! You have worked very hard to finish your book. It is amazing how quickly you got it finished. As you look at it and flip through the pages of this book with your name on it, you wonder "what now?" "How will I market this?" "Who is going to read it?" "How will anyone know about my book?"

Make sure you read Chapter 10 in *How to Write a Book ASAP*. There are many tips and ideas for you to use to get your book into the hands of others. There is one thing you need to remember once your book is published:

*No matter what publishing platform you use, you are going to have to market your book.*

You can either outsource your marketing (which can be expensive) or figure it out yourself (which will help you out in the long run).

If you are already a member of the *How to Write a Book ASAP* online training course, then you have access to in-depth marketing tools. Make sure you access the course and additional bonus courses, if you haven't done so already, by going to HowToWriteABookASAP.com/training.

If you want to have a greater chance of building a solid, ongoing relationship of trust with your readers, you need to establish yourself as a credible, trusted authority in your market. The more enthusiastic readers you have, the more credible you will become.

Take a little more time to work through the last exercise of this book. This will help guide you through the marketing process. You have some choices to make and now is the time to find the right fit for you.

*You have done something fantastic – you have written a book!*

*Take a moment to realize what an incredible accomplishment that is – you did it!*

*Congratulations!*

**Ten Ways to Build a Following**

Make sure you have read Chapter 10 in *How to Write a Book ASAP*. It is assumed that you understand what each of the following involves based on your reading. You need to choose at least two of these strategies to implement in order to build relationships with your readers. There is a place for notes after each one listed. Choose what is comfortable for you and start formulating a plan!

❖ **Email Marketing**

> ➤ Email marketing is highly scalable
> ➤ Email marketing is personal
> ➤ You can automate many tasks with your auto-responder
> ➤ Email marketing acts as a good pre-sell
> ➤ Email also works well to sell more
> ➤ Don't worry about subscribers unsubscribing

*Tips:*
- Keep in touch with your mailing list often
- Ask about their needs and concerns
- Send them gifts sometimes
- Be personal
- Be educational

Notes:

_____

_____

_____

❖ **Webinars**

*Audio-Visual*

> ➤ Organize
> ➤ Prepare
> ➤ Engage
> ➤ Teach
> ➤ Follow-up

Notes:

_____

_____

_____

_____

❖ **Teleseminars**

*Audio*

  ➢ Organize
  ➢ Prepare
  ➢ Engage
  ➢ Teach
  ➢ Follow-up

Notes:

_____

_____

_____

_____

❖ **Social Media**

  ➢ Be consistent
  ➢ Be authentic
  ➢ Be conversational
  ➢ Be informative
  ➢ Be engaging
  ➢ Don't be all about the numbers
  ➢ Don't be salesy
  ➢ Don't be fake
  ➢ Don't be impolite
  ➢ Don't spam
  ➢ Don't give up!

Notes:

_____

_____

_____

_____

❖ **Direct Mail**

➢ Create the "WOW" factor
➢ Build positive relationships

Notes:

_____

_____

_____

_____

❖ **Magazine**

➢ Be consistent in creation and distribution
➢ Choose print or email format
➢ Deliver valuable content

Notes:

_____

_____

_____

_____

❖ **Podcasts**

➢ Great if you don't like being in front of a camera
➢ Audio RSS feed

Notes:

_____

_____

_____

_____

_____

❖ **Applications**

➢ Mobile applications
➢ Desktop applications
➢ Social Media applications
➢ Browser applications

Notes:

_____

_____

_____

_____

❖ **Live Streaming Video**

➢ Takes more technological know-how
➢ Create a webcast
➢ Talk about whatever you like
➢ Extremely powerful

Notes:

_____

_____

_____

_____


❖ **Live Events**

➤ Most effective way to build relationships
➤ Face to Face
➤ Expensive
➤ Takes time and planning

Notes:

_____

_____

_____

_____


*Writing a book is simply a process, much like baking a cake. You put the effort and correct ingredients in and the end result is a beautiful, delicious and rewarding prize.*

# NOTES

# NOTES

# Continuing Education

Although much was discussed in the book *How to Write a Book ASAP*, I would like to continue working with you in your quest to finish your book.

As your personal coach, I will take you by the hand and guide you step-by-step through the intimidating and often confusing process of writing your first book.

As a valuable member of my How to Write a Book ASAP Online Training Course, you will receive exclusive and instant access to me, Garrett Pierson, as your mentor. You will also receive this workbook and several volumes of comprehensive, step-by-step video training guides.

Visit **HowToWriteABookASAP.com/Training** today to find out more!

To claim your discount, simply
Scan the QR code above or type this URL
into your browser –
**HowToWriteABookASAP.com/Training**

**What are you waiting for?
Let's get started today.**

www.ingramcontent.com/pod-product-compliance
Lightning Source LLC
LaVergne TN
LVHW081321060426
835509LV00015B/1624